TRAINS AND REAL LOCOMOTIVES

By Bill Trombello

Illustrated by Brian Diskin

TRAINS AND REAL LOCOMOTIVES

Copyright ©2010

Library of Congress Cataloging-in-Publication Data
Trombello, William,
Trains and Real Locomotives/ William Trombello
ISBN: 978-0-9842998-3-6
Juvenile

Copyright Registered: 2010
Published by Technical Training Consultants Inc. in the USA
801 Warrenville Rd.
Suite 222
Lisle, IL 60532
www.ttc-train.com
January 2010

TRAINS AND REAL LOCOMOTIVES

This book is dedicated to Mr. Jim Danielwicz, Vice President Mechanical for the Canadian National Railroad, and to his managers, supervisors, mechanics, electricians, and carman who keep the railroad running 365 days a year.

It's early morning when engineer Obie arrives at the locomotive shop. A locomotive shop is some times called a "Round House." That's because many years ago these buildings had a "turn table" that would turn locomotives around.

Engineer Obie walks into the shop to check on the locomotive that will be used to pull his train.

Mechanic Mike will perform an inspection on the locomotive that will pull engineer Obie's train.

Mike's inspecting key parts of the locomotive's big diesel engine.
Engineer Obie's train will stop if the diesel engine quits running.

Engineer Obie uses a "Switcher" locomotive to put his train together. To put a train together is sometimes called "Switching". This is how the little "Switcher" locomotive got its name. The switcher locomotive is too small to travel long distances, so the switcher locomotive stays near the railroad yard.

Engineer Obie backs up the little switcher with Carl the carmans' help.
A carman helps the engineer couple the cars together.

A railroad yard is a very dangerous place. To protect himself, Carl the carman wears a hard hat to protect his head, safety glasses to protect his eyes, ear plugs to protect his hearing, steel toed shoes to protect his feet, gloves to protect his hands, and a bright colored vest.

Carl always allows plenty of space when walking around stopped railroad cars. When crossing the railroad tracks, Carl would never ever step on the slippery rail.

An SD locomotive will pull engineer Obie's train. SD stands for "Super Duty". The SD locomotive has six traction motors that can pull heavy trains over long distances. Count the wheels on each side of the locomotive. Six wheels on each side and it's Super Duty!

Engineer Obie would use a GP locomotive to pull smaller trains. GP stands for "General Purpose." The GP locomotive has only four traction motors. Once again, count the wheels on each side of the locomotive. Four wheels on each side and it's General Purpose!

Engineer Obie would use an F40 locomotive to pull passenger cars. The "F" refers to the body style, and the 40 refers to the model type. The F40 can travel at very high speeds and also provides light and heat for the passenger cars.

Engineer Obie backs up the big SD locomotive and couples it to the train.

Trains today rarely use a caboose. The "End of the Train Detector" replaces the caboose.

Engineer Obie advances the throttle handle and the train leaves the railroad yard.

When the train goes over a hill or mountain the railroad cars climbing the hill are stretched apart and the railroad cars going down the hill are bunched together.

Sometimes this can cause the coupler between cars to break.

When a coupler breaks, the train will split apart and go into what we call "Emergency". Emergency prevents the locomotive from pulling, while brakes push against the wheels to stop the train.

Brakeman Bob rides in the locomotive with engineer Obie. A brakeman fixes broken couplers.

Locomotives blast their loud horns at all railroad crossings.

After a long journey, the train finally arrives at the next railroad yard.

The tired train crew walks across the street to the hotel for a good night's sleep. Tomorrow engineer Obie will drive a different train home.

ALSO BY WILLIAM TROMBELLO

THE WILLOW FALLS CHRISTMAS TRAIN

HOW A REAL LOCOMOTIVE WORKS